Understanding Your Life and Health Insurance

By

Olayinka Brimoh

M.Sc., MBA, CIM, CFP

Mortgage Broker, Chartered Investment Manager and Certified Financial Planner

TABLE OF CONTENTS

3. Chapter 2: Permanent Life Insurance

- Universal Life Insurance
  * Investments within universal life insurance.
  * Cost of insurance
- Limited Pay Policy
  * Types of limited pay policies
- Non-Participating Whole Life Policy
  - Features of non-participating - whole life insurance.
- Participating Whole Life - insurance.
  * Wealth
  * Estate
  * Features of participating whole life policy
  * Premium types
  * Dividend options
  * Additional deposit option
  * Coverage options
  * Premium offset
  * Additional benefits (riders)

9. Chapter 8: Real Estate or Participating Whole Life Insurance as an Alternative Investment.

- o Cost of owning real estate.
- o Benefits of real estate to an investor.
- o Cost of owning a participating whole life insurance.
- o Benefit of a participating whole life insurance to an investor
- o Tax implications:
  - a. Real estate.
  - b. Participating whole life insurance.

* Conclusion
* I am a life insurance policy

LEGAL PAGE

This book is to provide a guide to a better understanding of life and health insurance. It is by no means a recommendation of suitability of insurance products mentioned to the readers.

Author:
Olayinka Brimoh
Email:
olayinka.brimoh@valuesfinancial.ca
204-417-1938/204-880-9796
www.valuesfinancial.ca

Published by:
10:10:10 Publishing
Markham, ON. Canada

ABOUT THE AUTHOR

Olayinka is a financial and wealth planner with Values Financial Services Inc. He holds two master degrees in Agricultural Economics (M.Sc.) and Business Administration (MBA). He also holds two professional designations as Certified Financial Planner (CFP) and Chartered Investment Manager (CIM).

Olayinka started his career as a financial advisor with Sun Life Financial where he worked for five years. He received several industry recognitions and accolades, such as Advisor of the Year 2013, Health Advisor of the Year 2013, Runner-up Advisor of the Year in 2011 and 2012, Runner-up Recruit of the Year, 2009 and 2010, and Growth Award 2011. He also qualified for 16 consecutive tri-annual campaigns, the prestigious Sun Life President Circle, three consecutive elite conventions, four consecutive Sun Life annual conventions for top advisors, and MDRT since 2012.

Olayinka left Sun Life in May 2014 as the leading insurance and health advisor in Manitoba and one of the top 20 advisors in Canada. He founded Values Financial Services Inc., a full-range financial and mortgage Services Company in May 2014. He has since received industry recognitions in two consecutive qualifications to the elite 30 conference in 2014 – 2015 and 2015 – 2016, and two consecutive qualifications to the President Circle Conference 2014 – 2015 and 2015 – 2016.

He is married to his beloved wife, Elizabeth and they are blessed with two sons, *Temidayo* and *Oluwatosin*. Olayinka is also a Mortgage Broker, Real Estate Investor, Property Manager and a Farmer. His other interests include Human Rights,

Soccer, Economy, and the Capital Market.

Please visit us, at www.valuesfinacial.ca or Call: 204-417-1938 (business), or 204-880-9796 (mobile) *for a free non-obligation consultation.* ***I can help!***

ACKNOWLEDGMENT

Glory and honor to the Almighty God for giving me the grace to write this book. I am deeply indebted to all my clients for their support, encouragement and love in shaping me to be the financial planner that I am today. I am also grateful to all those who did not give me any chance to succeed and those who 'closed the doors' in my face when I tried to prospect them. I am what I am today because of you all.

Kudos to the insurance companies and the industry regulators for the structures, they have put in place. I acknowledge Wikipedia.org and CLHIA for the wonderful materials they published on insurance. I thank my past and present teachers, mentors, advisers and well-wishers for their constructive criticisms and advice.

Lastly, I would like to thank someone who I consider to be my rock, my amazing wife, Elizabeth Brimoh and my two sons, Temidayo and Tosin Brimoh for their support all the time.

FOREWORD

Olayinka Brimoh is one of the most experienced, knowledgeable, thorough and planned out insurance and financial minds whom I have had the pleasure to sit down and talk with. It is truly special and refreshing to have someone who care so much about their profession and the people that they work with like Olayinka does. It is only natural that Olayinka has taken his passion, experience, and knowledge and written a book dedicated to helping you to make important decisions about life and health insurance.

Understanding Your Life and Health Insurance is a comprehensive and thought out information guide on insurance. I strongly recommend reading this book when you are looking into life and health insurance. It weighs out the pros and cons of the often confusing and grey areas of insurance and explains everything you need to know in a clear and easy to understand way. In this book, Olayinka shares his top-notch knowledge and insider secrets that he has been using to aid his clients for years. Before making any decision on life and health insurance, you need to read this book.

Olayinka has accumulated many awards and accolades in the field throughout his long and prestigious career in the field and he shares his experiences with you. After reading Understanding Your Life and Health Insurance you will have the necessary information and understanding when making one of the most important investments in your life.

Raymond Aaron
New York Times Best-selling Author

INTRODUCTION

Insurance can be defined as the act, system or business of providing financial protection for property, life, health, e.t.c. against specified contingencies such as death, disability, illness, fire, burglary, loss or damage and involving payment of regular premium in return for a policy guaranteeing such protection.

Lloyd describe insurance as the main way for businesses and individuals to reduce the financial impact of a risk occurring.

Insurance can be sub-divided into different categories such as life, health, accidental, auto and property insurance.

This book will focus on the life and health insurance sub-divisions, its features and the different types of such insurance.

Ancient World

According to Wikipedia.org, insurance dates from early human society. There were two types of economies in human societies: natural or non-monetary economies which use barter and trade with no centralized or standardized set of financial instruments, and monetary economies with markets, currency and financial instruments. Insurance in the former case entails agreements of mutual aid, for example, if one family's house was destroyed, the neighbors were committed in helping to rebuild it. Granaries embodied another early form of insurance to indemnify against famines.

The first methods of transferring or distributing risk in a monetary economy were practiced by Chinese and Babylonian traders in the 3rd and 2nd millennia B.C. respectively. Chinese merchants traveling treacherous rivers would redistribute their wares across many vessels to limit the loss due to any single vessel capsizing.

The Babylonians developed a system which was recorded in the famous Code of Hammurabi, c.1750BC, and was practiced by early Mediterranean sailing merchants. If a merchant received a loan to fund his shipment, he would pay the lender an additional sum in exchange for the lender's guarantee to cancel the loan should the shipment be lost or stolen at sea.

Achaemenian monarchs in ancient Persia were presented with annual gifts from various ethnic groups under their control. This would function as an early form of political insurance and officially bound the Persian monarch to protect the group from harm.

In 1st millennium B.C. the inhabitants of Rhodes created the general average.

This allowed groups of merchants to pay to insure their goods while shipping them together. The collected premiums would be used to reimburse any merchant whose goods were jettisoned during transport, whether by storm or sink-age.

The ancient Athenian 'maritime loan' advanced money for voyages with repayment collected if the ship was lost. In the 4th century B.C. loan rates differed according to perceived danger of making a voyage that time of the year which implied an intuitive pricing of risk with an effect similar to insurance.

The Greeks and Romans introduced the origins of life and health insurance in 600 B.C. when they created guilds which were also known as 'benevolent societies'. These were used to care for the families of deceased members, as well as paying the funeral expenses of members. Guilds in the middle ages served similar purposes.

The Jewish Talmud also dealt with several aspects of insuring goods. Before insurance was established in the late 17th century, there were 'friendly societies' that existed in England, these groups donated a certain amount of money to a general sum, which could be used for emergencies.

Medieval Era

Separate insurance contracts (i.e. insurance policies not bundled with loan or other kinds of contracts) were invented in Genoa in the 14th century, as were insurance pools which were backed by pledges of landed estates. The first known insurance contract dates from Genoa in 1347, and in the next century maritime insurance developed widely. Premiums now were intuitively varied with risks.

These new insurance contracts allowed insurance to be separated from investment, a separation of roles that first proved useful in marine insurance. The first printed book on insurance was legal treatise on *insurance and merchant's bets* by Pedro de Santarem, written in 1488 and published in 1552.

Modern Insurance

Insurance became more sophisticated in the Enlightenment era of Europe, and specialized varieties developed. Different forms of insurance developed in London in the early decades of the 17th century, for example the will of the English colonist Robert Hayman which mentioned two *'Policies of Insurance'* which was taken out with the diocesan Chancellor of London Arthur Duck, which was valued at 100 pounds each. One was related to the safe arrival of Hayman's ship in Guyana and the other to 'one hundred pounds assured by the said Doctor Arthur Duck on my life' (will of Robert Hayman, 1682 records of the prerogative court of Canterbury, Catalogue Reference PROB 11/63).

Property Insurance

Property insurance as we know today can be traced to the Great Fire of London, which in 1666 devoured more than 13,000 houses. The devastating effects of the fire converted the development of insurance "from a matter of convenience into one of urgency, a change of opinion reflected in Sir Christopher Wren's inclusion of a site for 'The Insurance Office' in his new plan for London in 1667 (Dickson 1960)." In 1681, the first fire insurance company was established by the economist Nicholas Barbon and 11 associates called 'Insurance Office for Houses' at the back of the Royal Exchange to insure brick and frame houses, it initially insured 5000 houses.

In the wake of this successful venture many similar companies were founded in the following decades. Initially, each company employed its own fire department to prevent and minimize the damage from conflagrations on the properties that were insured by them. They also began to issue 'fire insurance marks' to their customers. These would be displayed prominently above the main door of the property and allowed the insurance company to identify properties that had taken out insurance with them. One such notable company was the Hand in Hand Fire and Life Insurance Society which was founded in 1696 at Tom's Coffeehouse in St. Martin's Lane in London.

In Colonial America the first insurance company that underwrote fire insurance was formed in modern day Charleston, South Carolina in 1732. Benjamin Franklin helped to popularize and made standard practice of insurance particularly property insurance. He founded the Philadelphia contributorship for insurance of houses from loss by fire in 1752.

Life Insurance

The first life insurance policies were taken out in the early 18th century. The first company to offer life insurance was the Amicable Society for a Perpetual Assurance Office which was founded in the year 1706 in London, England by William Talbot and Sir Thomas Allen. The first plan of life insurance was that each member paid a certain annual payment per share on one to three shares with consideration to age of the members being 12-55. At the end of the year, a portion of the 'amicable contribution' was divided among the wives and children of deceased members and it was in proportion to the amount of shares the heirs owned.

Amicable Society started with 2000 members. The first life table was written by Edmund Halley in 1693, but it was only in the 1750s that the necessary mathematical and statistical tools were in place for the development of modern life insurance. James Dodson, a mathematician and actuary tried to establish a new company that issued premiums aimed at correctly offsetting the risks of long-term life assurance policies after being refused admission to the Amicable Life Assurance Society because of his advanced age. He was unsuccessful in his attempt at procuring a charter from the government before his death in 1757.

His disciple, Edward Rowe Mores was finally able to establish the Society for Equitable Assurances on Lives and Survivorship in 1762. It was the world's first mutual insurer and it pioneered age-based premiums based on mortality rate laying 'the framework for scientific insurance practice and development' and the basis of modern life insurance on which all life insurance schemes were subsequently based.

Mores also specified that the chief official should be called an actuary, the earliest known references to the position as a business was concerned. The first modern actuary was William Morgan who was appointed in 1775 and served until 1830. In 1776, the society carried out the first actuarial valuation of liabilities and subsequently distributed the first reversionary bonus (1781) and interim bonus (1809) among its members. It also used regular valuations to balance competing interests. The society sought to treat its members equitably and the directors tried to ensure that the policy holders received a fair return on their respective investments. Premiums were regulated according to age and anyone could be admitted regardless of their state of health or other circumstances. The sale of life insurance in the United States of America (USA) began in the late 1760s. The Presbyterian Synods in Philadelphia and New York founded the Corporation for Relief of Poor and Distressed Widows and Children of Presbyterian Ministers in 1759. Episcopalian priests created a comparable relief fund in 1769, and in 1837 more than two dozen life insurance companies were started, but fewer than half a dozen survived.

Accident Insurance

Accident insurance became available in the 19th century. It was comparable to the modern day disability insurance. The pioneers of accident insurance were the Railway Passengers Assurance Company which was formed in 1848 in England to insure the then rising numbers of fatalities on the newly constructed railway system.

It was registered as the Universal
Casualty Compensation Company the
company sold the accident insurance
through the railway companies by
travel ticket sales.

Insurance in Canada

In the mid-1830s, some parishes and
municipalities in Lower and Upper
Canada offered fire insurance. The
first Canadian life insurance company
was founded in Hamilton, Ontario in
1847. Formation of major companies
such as Mutual life, Sun Life,
Confederation Life and London Life,
in the mid-1870s prompted the passing
of the first Canadian insurance law in
1868. The industry has evolved over
the years with industrialization and
advancement in technology. Many new
products were gradually introduced
into the Canadian market and many
other companies were formed.

Underlying Principle of Insurance

Insurance is a written agreement between the insured and the insurer. The insurer promises to take the specified risk with some applied conditions of the insured for a consideration call premium. The underlying principle is the law of volume (large number), which states that with the increasing number of risk and exposure, the actual losses approach their expected values quite closely. The expected collective loss is then shared proportionally by all the insured in the form of premiums.

Operation of Insurance

Most insurance companies are stock and mutual companies. Stock companies are profit-oriented and widely owned by shareholders while mutual companies are owned by the insurer. Any excess of income over claim settlement and expenses are returned to the insured in the form of dividends or reduced premiums.

Government-operated agencies like workers' compensation, automobile insurance and some pension plans also provide protections which were mandatory against certain risks. Such agreements are termed 'Social Insurance'.

Such programs do not necessarily operate on the express assumption that sufficient funds are accumulated in advance for the payment of losses. The payments of claims are usually made from the general tax revenues.

Supervision and Regulation

There are many reasons why the insurance industry is regulated. For example, premiums are paid in advance by the insured and benefit may be paid in the far distant future to the insured, which has little or no power to protect his/her interests. In addition to the self-regulation through industry associations, the responsibility for the supervision of insurance in Canada is shared by both the federal and provincial governments.

The federal department of insurance is responsible for the regulation and licensing of federally-registered companies and is concerned with their ability to meet the obligations of policy holders. This is accomplished by solvency tests that are requested from insurance companies to submit financial statements to establish that they have sufficient financial resources. The provincial superintendents of insurance prescribe statutory contract conditions which regulate the licensing of the agents, brokers, etc.

Insurance Products

A large number of insurance protections are available, for example, life insurance which provides financial resources to support the survivors of the insured or to pay the obligations (credit insurance) in case of the death of the breadwinner. Term insurance protects against the risks of premature death during a specified term; whole life insurance pays the face amount of the policy whenever the insured dies. Disability insurance protects against the loss of income due to a disability. Other types of insurance are health insurance, liability insurance, automobile insurance and property insurance. This book would focus on life insurance, critical illness insurance, personal health insurance, long-term care insurance, disability insurance and accidental death insurance.

Assuris

Assuris was founded in 1990; it is a non-profit organization that protects Canadian policy holders in the event that their life insurance company fails. Assuris' role is to protect policy holders by minimizing the loss of benefits and ensuring a quick transfer of their coverage to another company in good standing and to ensure that their protected benefit continues. Every life insurance company in Canada is required by the federal, provincial or territorial regulators to become a member of Assuris.

Assuris is designated by the Federal Minister of Finance under the Insurance Companies Act of Canada and specified in the Quebec Reglement d'application de la Loi sur les assurances.

In the event a life insurance company becomes insolvent, the policies written by that company will be transferred to a solvent company. Assuris guarantees that the insured would retain at least 85% of the benefit promised by the insolvent company www.assuris.ca. Such benefits include monthly income, health expenses, death benefits and cash values.

Deposits held in the insolvent life insurance company are also transferred to a company in good standing and Assuris guarantees that such deposits have 100% of the accumulated values of up to $100,000. Deposit includes dividend deposit accounts, universal life overflow accounts, and accumulation annuities.

Insurance products and deposits protected by Assuris include the following:

Insurance Products:
- Life Insurance
- Critical Illness insurance
- Health Expenses
- Disability Income
- Long-term Care
- Group Insurance
- Segregated funds
- Annuities

Deposits
- Accumulation Annuities
- Group Retirement
- TFSA

CHAPTER ONE

Term Life Insurance
(If I Die Insurance)

Life insurance is a contract between the insured and the insurer, where the insurer promises to pay the designated beneficiary (or beneficiaries) a sum of money (the benefit or face amount) in exchange for a premium upon the death of the insured.
Life insurance falls into two major categories:

- **Protection (pure insurance) policies:** These are the easiest types of insurance to understand. The insurer promises the insured that a specified amount of money will be paid in the event of death, in exchange for a premium. Examples are term insurance and accidental life insurance.
- **Investment policies:** The objectives of these types of

policies are to facilitate growth of capital. Examples are participating whole insurance and universal life.

Term Life Insurance

Term life insurance provides life insurance coverage for a specified length of time. This is a pure insurance; the policy does not accumulate cash value as there is no investment. This type of insurance can be casually described as a situation where one uses premium to buy a certain amount of insurance for a specified period of time. There are different types of term insurance. The most common are the 10, 20, 25, 30 terms insurance. T-100 is another type of term insurance.

There are three main factors to consider, when considering term insurance:

1. Amount of insurance needed (the face amount or the death benefit).

2. The amount of premium to be paid (cost of insurance).
3. The length of coverage.

Common Uses of Term Insurance

Term insurance can be described as the 'if' insurance. It is commonly used to cover short-term or medium-term debts like line of credit, credit cards, car loans and business debt. It can also be used to cover long-term debt, such as mortgages.

Term insurance is also used for income replacement if the insured dies, the beneficiary would receive the death benefit and invest such, for a steady flow of cash to replace the income of the insured.

Features of Term Insurance
The common features of term life insurance are:
1. **Renewability:** This feature allows the insured to maintain the same

amount of insurance coverage without having to provide further medical sample or asked medical questions, till expiry for a higher premium on renewals.

2. **Convertibility:** This feature enables the insured to convert the term insurance to a permanent insurance without having to provide evidence of insurability. This feature with most companies expires at age of 70.

3. **Expiry:** Term insurance expires at age 85 with most companies. However, some term insurance expires at age 65, 70, some at 75 or 80.

4. **Term 10 Conversion:** Most companies allow holders of 10-year term life insurance to convert the term 10 policy to 20years term policy, within the first 5 years of the policies without evidence of insurability.

5. **Premium Increases:** Term insurance has low premium at the beginning however, the premium increases upon renewals. Premium is level during term for example; the premium for a 20-year term insurance remains the same for the first 20 years and increase in the 21st year.

Illustration of Term Life Insurance

All life insurance companies offer term insurance at a competitive rate. The premium for term insurance, like all other types of insurance depends on factors like the age, health, gender, family history, driving record, etc. For a 35-year-old male regular health, non-smoker, $500,000 insurance, the premium for 20 years currently ranges from $35.64 to $60.75 for both medical and non-medical insurance. However, the premium should not be the only consideration when choosing the right insurance. I recommend that you contact a trained professional with a CFP (*Certified Financial Planner*) designation, for your insurance needs.

Please note that the premium and the face amount quoted above are guarantees for 20 years. Typically for a term insurance, the premium increase on renewals is usually by 15 folds or by 1500%. A $36.72 monthly premium at age 35 could increase to $572.39 monthly payment at age 55 (and for another 20 years).

Graphic illustration of a 20-years term insurance increase.

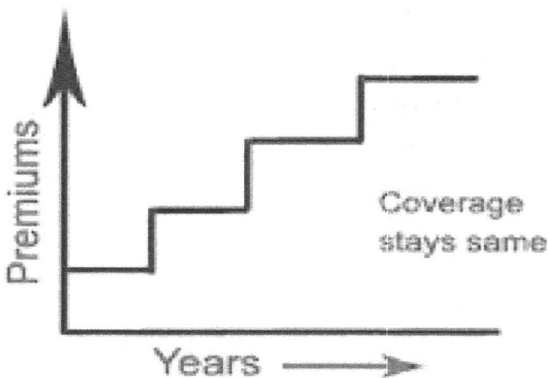

Insurance

Some factors determine the eligibility of clients for life insurance. Some of them are as follows:

1. Criminal record/ prison time.
2. Driving under the influence (alcohol, drugs).
3. Bankruptcy record.
4. Impeding foreign and past foreign travelling
5. Scheduled/recommended medical test/ pending result or exams.
6. Income level and sources of income.
7. Residency status.
8. Job hazard/ employment type.
9. Aviation activities.
10. Recreational activities like aerial activity, mountain climbing, etc.
11. Alcohol consumption.
12. Smoking status and consumption
13. Family medical record.

14. General state of health.
15. BMI (Body Mass Index).
16. Amount of insurance currently owned (group inclusive).

Term Insurance vs. Mortgage Protection
(Creditor protection)

Lenders often request that the borrowers have a protection on the loan(s) they provided. The creditor protection is not the same as a life insurance. The differences are as follows:

1. The lender as the beneficiary: With a creditor protection or mortgage life insurance, the creditor is the named beneficiary for the loan balance in the event of the death of the insured.

2. Coverage amount is the balance of the loan on the date the insured dies, while term life

insurance allows for a fixed amount of coverage throughout the duration of the coverage.

3. The mortgage life insurance is not transferable from lender to lender, while term life insurance is portable and may even be used to protect future loans.

4. Mortgage life insurance cannot be converted or modified in any way, but term life insurance can be modified or converted to permanent life insurance.

5. Mortgage life insurance only cover the balance of the loan and once the loan is paid off the insurance is cancelled while, term insurance can be kept in-force till age 85, with most carriers or converted to perm anent life insurance.

6. With Mortgage life insurance the clients have no choice but with term insurance, the clients has the freedom to choose the insurance company they want to deal with, the amount of coverage they want, the duration of the coverage and the type (term or perm) they want.

7. With Mortgage life insurance clients do not have the opportunity of having a license life advisor to guide them on choices.

CHAPTER TWO

Permanent Life Insurance
(When I Die Insurance)

Permanent life insurance is life insurance that covers the remaining lifetime of the insured. I describe this type of insurance as 'when'. Permanent life insurance policy accumulates cash surrender values (CSV) up to its date of maturation. The owner can access the fund in cash values by withdrawing the cash, borrowing the cash or by surrendering the policy and receiving the surrendered value.

Permanent life insurance is considered to be insurance with investment. There are four basic types:
1. Universal life
2. Participating Whole Life permanent life

3. Non-Participating Permanent Whole Life Insurance
4. Limited pay

Universal Life Insurance

Universal Life insurance which is commonly called 'UL' is a relatively new insurance product. It combines permanent life with greater flexibility in premium payments with the potential for greater growth of cash values. There are several types and kinds of universal life insurance, including Variable Universal Life (VUL), guaranteed death benefit, equity-indexed universal life insurance, and the more traditional-fixed universal life insurance (interest-sensitive).

In universal life insurance, the premium gets paid into an investment 'account' that is expected to yield some positive returns, the premium tax cost of insurance and management expenses get deducted from the 'account'. The balance on such an account is referred to as the cash surrender value of the universal life policy. Universal life insurance, addresses the disadvantages of fixed-death benefit and the fixed premium of the non-participating whole life policy. In universal life insurance, both the premium and the death benefit are flexible.

Investment within Universal Life

There are varieties of investment to choose from in today's universal life. Some are:
1. Daily Interest Accounts.
2. Bond Accounts (Fixed Income Accounts).
3. GIC Accounts
4. Equity Index Account.
5. Equity Growth Account.
6. Strategic Equity Account.
7. Tactical Equity Account.

Cost of Insurance

There are different types of cost of insurance with Universal Life namely:

1. **Yearly renewable term of insurance:** With this cost of insurance, the cost of insurance increases every year till age 100.
2. **Yearly till 65, then level:** The cost of insurance increases yearly till age 65 before it levels till age 100.
3. **Yearly till 85, then level:** The cost of insurance increases yearly till age 85 and then levels from age 85 to age 100.
4. **Level:** The cost of insurance is level from day one till age 100.

Limited Pay Policy

The premium for a limited pay policy are usually paid off within a stipulated time frame like 10 years, 15 years, 20 years or till age 65. Limited pay policy can be a type of universal life policy or a type of whole life policy. At the expiration of the payment period limited pay policy leaves the policy holder with a guaranteed death benefit and no further premium to pay. Limited pay policy offers a guaranteed premium, guaranteed death benefit and fixed period of payment.

Types of Limited Pay Policies
The duration of payment differs among limited pay policies.
1. **Single Premium policy:** This type requires only one premium paid at policy inception.
2. **10 pay:** This type requires payment for 10 years.
3. **20 pay:** This type requires payment for 20 years.
4. **Pay till 65:** This type requires payment till age 65.

Non-Participating Whole Life Policy

This policy ensures that the insured party would have the insurance at the same cost till age 100 regardless of the investment return experience by the insurer. The return of investment of the insurer is not shared with the insured with this type of policy. Like all other types of insurance, the premium for this type of insurance is based on some factors as described (*see the eligibility of insurance in Chapter 1*).

Features of Non-Participating Whole Life

1. **Guaranteed premium:** The premium for this policy is guaranteed for life regardless of the changes in the investment experience of the insurer.
2. **Guaranteed Death Benefit:** The death benefit of this policy is guaranteed by the insurer for life.

3. **Guaranteed cash value:** The cash value for this type of policy is guaranteed by the insurer and it is not tied to the investment returns of the insurer. The cash value usually starts to accrue during the 8th year that the policy is in force.

Participating Whole Life Policy

This type of policy entitles the owner to share in the profit (dividend) of the insurer. The profit is paid annually by dividend to the insured. Both types allow the owner of the policy to make cash withdrawals or take policy loans from the policy.

1. **Wealth:** This type of participating whole life provides permanent insurance protection but focuses on higher cash values over the short-term, in exchange for modest long-term growth.

This type of policy is good for you, if:

a. You are interested in accessing the cash values in the early years of the policy to finance your child's education, pay off debts and bridge retirement income while ensuring that there is a death benefit to protect your estate.

b. You are a small business owner with a need to protect your business from loss due to premature death, while ensuring you have some flexibility to meet the changing cash flows of your business.

2. **Estate:** The estate type provides permanent life insurance protection combined with long-term cash values and death benefit growth. This type of policy is good for you, if:

a. You have no immediate need of the cash values.
b. You would like to access the cash values in the future to supplement your retirement income.
c. You want cash values and death benefit growth over the long term.

Features of Participating Whole Life Insurance

1. Guaranteed Premium: The premium of this policy is guaranteed. The payer knows for certain the cost of the insurance.
2. Guaranteed Death Benefit: The base death benefit for this type of policy is guaranteed. However, the death benefit could increase depending on the dividend option selected.
3. Guaranteed Cash Values: This policy has guaranteed cash values built in the policy. This cash value

is payable regardless of whether a dividend is declared or not.

4. Premium Offset: This policy allows the owner to go on a dividend holiday, if the expected dividend is enough to cover the cost of insurance on the policy going forward.

Premium Types

There are two common premium types:

1. **Pay to age 100:** The premium for the policy is spread over the life time of the insured.
2. **20 pay:** The premium for the policy is paid off in the first 20 years of the policy.

Dividend Options

The insured can have the declared dividend paid in any of the following ways (the choice made, determine the long term value of the cash surrender values and the death benefit):

1. **Paid-up Additional Insurance:** Dividend credited to the policy is used to purchase additional insurance, which is paid up. This additional amount of insurance is also participating and it can also earn dividend and has a cash value. With compound growth your death benefit and cash value increases over time.

2. **Dividend on Deposit:** Dividend credited to the policy is automatically deposited into an account that is similar to a saving account, with the insurer. The insured can access the dividends account at any time. Dividend on deposit earns interest daily and is compounded annually at the insurer rate.

3. **Premium Reduction:** This option provides a cost-effective

way of paying the premium. The annual dividend is used to reduce the future year premium payments. If the dividend paid is in excess to the premium required, the excess would be deposited into the withdrawable premium funds (earns daily interest).

4. **Cash Payment:** This option gives you the opportunity to receive annual dividend in cash.

5. **Enhanced Coverage:** Each dividend is used to buy one-year term life insurance up to a permitted   maximum which is called the enhanced coverage amount. Any excess dividends are used to buy paid-up participating life insurance.

Additional Deposit Option

Additional deposit option allows clients to make extra deposit above the required premium, to help grow the long-term cash values in their participating life.

Availability: Additional deposit options are available for all ages on both 20-pay and limited pay premium options. Additional deposit option in the first policy year does not require medical requirements except if the policy is issued substandard.

Maximize Tax-Advantage Growth
Additional deposit option payments buy paid-up additional insurance to maximize growth.

- The paid-up addition adds to the non-guaranteed cash values of the policy.
- Both the basic insurance and the paid-up addition are eligible to earn dividends each year, which further accelerates the growth within the policy.
- With the paid-up additions dividend option, paid-up addition

will immediately increase the death benefit.

Maximum additional deposit option payment: The maximum limit on the additional deposit option maintains the policy's tax-exempt status.

- The maximum limit is calculated at policy issue based on the life insurer's sex, risk class, issue age, amount of coverage, plan types, premium option and the current dividend scale.
- Changes to the dividend scale and income tax act exempt regulations, as well as changes clients may request to their policy, which will affect the maximum additional deposit option payment limit.
- Insurers would not accept an additional deposit option payment that would cause the policy to lose its tax-exempt status.

Coverage Options
Single life:
- Coverage is based on one insured person.
- The death benefit is payable on the death of that insured person.

Joint first-to-die:
- Coverage is based on two insured persons.
- The death benefit is payable on the death of the first insured.

Joint last-to-die:
- Coverage is based on two insured persons.
- The death benefit is payable on the death of the last insured.
- Premium is payable to the death of the last insured or to the guaranteed premium payment option.
- At issue, the insured persons must be between ages 18-80 for the life time and ages 18-65 for the 20 pay.

Premium Offset

This is a non-contractual feature that may be available at some point in the future. Premium offset may occur when the policy yields dividends that are enough to cover the cost of insurance on an annual basis. This happens when the base amount and the paid-up addition insurance have created a base large enough to earn adequate dividends for the policy holder. If a client chooses paid-up addition as the dividend option, the potential premium offset may occur earlier than if they had selected enhanced insurance or any other dividend option. While premium offset offers clients future flexibility for premium payments, it is important to remember that other values, such as the increase in death benefit and cash values will not accumulate to the same extent as they would, if the client continued to pay the premium. The performance of the policy holder's dividends plays an important role in determining the future premium offset point. There are a number of other factors that should be taken into consideration. These factors include cash withdrawals, premium loans, policy loans, change in dividend option and the addition of optional benefits to the policy.

Additional benefits
These are available at issue with both the estate and the wealth plans.
1. **Term insurance benefit:** Each insured person with a basic insurance benefit can include a term benefit on themselves or on another person, such as a spouse, family member or business partner. The minimum face amount of the term insurance benefit allowed is $25,000 though some insurers allow up to a maximum of $10,000,000 coverage. The attached term benefit comes with the privilege of

renewals and conversions on or before the insured is 70 years old.

2. **Child term rider:** This benefit allows children and future children of the insured parent to be covered under the parent's life insurance policy until the child is 25 years old. The parent who is the base life insured must be between ages 16 and 55. The child term insurance benefit is available to the children born or legally adopted by the insured person, who are 18 years of age or younger at the time of application and a standard risk. Any children born or adopted after the date of application are automatically insured regardless of their risk class. Some insurers allow stepchildren at the time of application or supplementary application. The minimum amount is $10,000 and the maximum is $30,000. If the insured dies, the children are

covered under this benefit until age 25, or until they apply for a new life insurance policy as permitted under this benefit. Between their 18-25th birthday, children insured under this benefit will have the right to buy additional life insurance for up to five times the amount of the child term insurance. The child term insurance will end on either the child's 25th birthday or the policy anniversary nearest the insured person's 65th birthday, whichever date comes first.

3. **Accidental death benefit:** The accidental death benefit option pays out an additional death benefit to the beneficiary, if the insured person's death was due to an accident. The benefit is available on single life coverage option till age 70. The minimum ADB insurance amount is $10,000 and the

maximum amount is the policy face amount.

4. **Guaranteed Insurability Option (GIO):** Insured persons with the guaranteed insurability option can buy additional insurance without providing evidence of insurability. The insured with GIO has the option to purchase additional coverage every three years until 45-55 years of age depending on the insurer's terms.

5. **Total disability benefit:** This feature allows the insured to maintain coverage if they become totally disabled and are unable to earn income. The premium may not be waived if:
    i. The total disability continues for less than six months
    ii. The total disability resulted from self- inflicted injuries

iii. The total disability results from the committing of a criminal offence.
iv. The client must make the claim during the period of disability

CHAPTER THREE

Critical Illness Insurance
(If I'm Sick Insurance)

Critical illness insurance is an insurance coverage, in which the insurer makes a lump-sum cash payment to the insured in the event the insured is diagnosed with one of the specific illnesses on a predetermined list as contained in the insurance policy. Critical illness insurance can help bridge the often overlooked gap in insurance protection and help pay benefits for daily expenses, lifestyle changes and recovery expenses in the event of a covered illness. The right coverage can help the insured to focus on their health and worry less about expenses.

How Can Critical Illness Insurance Help?

Critical illness insurance can help you not to go into debt or prevent you from depleting your assets or withdrawing from your retirement savings. Critical illness insurance can be used in any of the following ways:

- **Reduce your financial burden:** Reduce debt and other money related concerns while you cope with your illness. Pay off or reduce your mortgage, credit cards or other debts or help keep your business running.

- **Focus on recovery:** Replace or supplement any reduction or loss of income for you and your spouse (family), who may take time off work to care for you. This allows you to spend more time with your family or friends.

- **Access cutting–edge medical services and treatments:**

Provide resources for medical treatments and medication that are not covered by the government and private health care plans. If the critical illness happens to you outside of Canada, the insurance can help pay for treatment that may not be available in such jurisdictions, and can offset the cost of family travel and lodging expenses.

- **Maintain your independence:** To cover the cost of bringing in domestic help (care giver/ home care attendant) for you and your family. Modify your home or vehicle to improve your mobility.

Probability of a Critical Illness

Many of us know of friends, family, co-workers or neighbors who have suffered or survived a critical illness, but we often think it cannot happen to us. Take a careful look at the statistics. Critical illness can happen to anyone.

1. It is estimated that there are over 70,000 heart attacks in Canada every year about 192 cases per day!
2. An estimated 3,075 Canadians will be diagnosed with cancer every week, or about 440 cases per day!
3. There are 50,000 cases of stroke in Canada each year with 75% left with disability. This is approximately 137 cases per day!
4. According to the Canadian Cancer Society (*www.cancer.ca*) one in three Canadians will develop a life-threatening cancer in their lifetime 33.3%!
5. One in two heart attack victims are under 65 years of age 50%. (Heart and stroke foundation (*www.heartandstroke.ca*).

Types of Plan

With most insurance companies in Canada, there are different types of plans, these are as follows:

- **Term 10:** This comes with a guaranteed premium for 10 years and guaranteed face amount until age 75. The premium increases every 10 years to reflect increase in risk. Typically coverage ends at age 75.

- **Term 20:** This comes with a guaranteed premium for 20 years and guarantee face amount until age 75. Premium increases every 20 years to reflect the change in risk. Coverage expires at age 75.

- **Term 75:** Term 75 comes with a flat premium guaranteed until the end of the policy and guaranteed face amount. Policy ends at age 75.

- **Term 100 or Permanent coverage:** This guarantees coverage at the same premium for a guaranteed face amount for the rest of the insured person's life.

Coverage

The following are the illnesses covered by most insurers in Canada. Please check with your advisor for:

* Cancer.
* Heart attack.
* Stroke.
*Acquired brain injury.
* Alzheimer's disease.
* Aortic surgery.
* Aplastic anemia.
* Bacterial meningitis.
*Benign brain tumour.
* Blindness.
* Coma.
* Coronary artery.
* Bypass surgery.
* Deafness.
*Heart valve replacement.
* Kidney failure.
* Occupational HIV infection.

Severe burns.
Paralysis.
Parkinson's disease.
Multiple sclerosis.
Motor neuron disease.
Major organ transplant.
Loss of limbs.
Major organ failure on waiting list.
Loss of speech.

Additional benefits (riders) of Critical illness insurance

The critical illness insurance has the following additional benefits (riders) that insured persons can choose from:

- Disability waiver.
- Return of premium on death.
- Return of premium on cancelation or expiration (15 years, 20 years, 25 years, 65 years or 75 years).
- Loss of independence existence.
- Long term care conversion option.

Disability Waiver (DW): If the insured becomes totally disabled and the disability continues for more than six consecutive months, they may qualify for the waiver of premium (stop paying premiums) for the duration of the disability.

Return of Premium on death (ROPD): The premiums paid by the insured would be paid to the named beneficiary 100% in the event the insured person dies while the policy is still in effect.

Return of Premium on Cancellation (ROPC): With the return of premium on cancellation, the insurer will return the entire premium paid by the insurer at a pre-determined number of years. There are options for the insured to choose from with many insurers. Some of these options are:

- Return of premiums on cancellation after 15 years (100%).
- Return of premiums on cancellation 100% after 15 years, or 75% after 10 years.
- Return of premiums on cancellation 100% after 15 years, or 50% after 10 years.
- Return of premiums on cancellation 100% after 20 years, or 50% after 10 years.

- Return of premiums on cancellation 100% after 25 years, or 50% after 10 years.
- Return of premiums on cancellation 100% at age 65.
- Return of premiums on expiry at age 75 (for term 75).

Loss of Independence existence: the insured has coverage for loss of independent existence (as contained in the policy).

Long-term care Conversion: The insured with this option has the privilege to convert the critical illness insurance to a long-term care insurance policy without providing evidence of insurability.
This rider can be exercised between the client's 60th birthday and 65th birthday.

CHAPTER FOUR
Disability Insurance
(If I Can't Work Due To Injury or Illness Insurance)

Disability Insurance (DI) is an income replacement plan. The insured gets a steady stream of income (the face amount) from the insurer if they cannot work due to injury or illness as covered under the term of agreement of the policy for a specified period of time. Disability could be a result of degenerative condition or sudden incident. It could be due to mental illness, sport injury or another form of illness and injury.

Need for Disability Insurance
Most people recognize the need for life insurance but struggle to understand why they should protect their income with disability insurance. Disability insurance is a type of insurance that

protects your income should you have a disability and are not able to work. The fact is that when you are disabled because of an injury or illness your income stops but not your bills and expenses.

Fact:
1. One in three people on average will be disabled for 90 days or more before age 65.
2. Disability can last longer than expected; it may last months, even years.

Sources of Disability Insurance

Disability benefits replace about 60-85% of regular income. Some plans are tax-free while others are taxable. It is possible to receive benefits from more than one source but the principle of coordination of insurance applies, to forestall a situation where the benefits are more than the income.

The sources of disability plans are:
1. Government plan

2. Group (Employer) plan
3. Private or individual plan.
Some other sources are creditor
insurance (e.g. mortgage protection,
credit card protection), auto insurance
plan and long-term or critical illness
plans.

Individual Plans

According to the CLHIA close to 1
million Canadians have their own
policies arranged through life and
health insurance agents. There are
advantages to owning an individual
disability plan; group plans end when
you change jobs or leave the
professional/trade association while an
individual plan does not end when
career changes are made. Individual
plans are tax free because the premium
is paid with the after-tax income of an
individual tax payer. An individual
plan can be tailored to meet the
specific needs of the insured, such as

own occupation, benefit period, inflation protection, etc.

Types of Individual Plans

Non-cancellable: The price and the policy cannot be changed during the contract period as specified on the policy. It is also called non-cancellable guaranteed renewable.

Guaranteed renewable: This means that the insurance company must renew the policy but the premium can be raised for everyone in certain class or category (according to the occupation).

Commercial: The insurer can decide to cancel the contract on the anniversary of the contract, or they can make some modification to the contract as a result of any previous claim.

Riders (additional benefits) of disability plans

These are some of the additional benefits to individual disability plans:

1. **Own Occupation:** This benefit enables the insured to be paid if, due to illness and or injury, they cannot perform the duties of their own occupation. This is a very important rider for professionals and others in specialized occupations.
2. **Residual disability:** The insured would receive claim from the insurer if they can go back to work and are not able to work as much as they were before. Residual disability is proportionate to the earning power lost, regardless of the number of hours worked. For example, if the insured suffers a 65% loss of pre-disability income loss due to illness and/or injury, they would receive 65% of the total disability benefit for as long as they are disabled (up to the maximum specified in the policy).

3. **Partial disability:** The benefit to be paid would be determined by the loss of time on the job. Generally, most insurers pay 50% of the total disability benefit for a short period of time (6-12 months) regardless of the percentage of lost earnings.

4. **Future Insurability option:** Due to rising income during the course of a career. The insured with this rider can buy more disability without showing new medical evidence.

5. **Cost of living benefit:** This rider helps to index the benefit to inflation. It acts as a hedge to inflation.

6. **Catch-up:** This rider provides the insured with a lump sum payment equal to the amount not paid during the waiting period of

the policy, should the client become totally disabled for a period of at least 180 consecutive days. This rider enables the insured to 'financially catch up' from the impact of disability (up to the maximum specified in the policy).

7. **Expense equalizer rider:** This rider helps the insured with a longer waiting period by providing payment for them to cover their expenses (like mortgage, rent, car loan, lease payment, line of credit) during the waiting period before the disability payment commences.

8. **Sale of business facilitator rider:** If an insured business owner has to sell their interest in their business due to disability (injury and/ or illness), this rider

entitles them to payments to cover legal and accounting fees.

9. **First day accident rider:** This rider technically eliminates the waiting period and pays for the disability benefit from the first day of a disability due to an injury, regardless of where it happens.

10. **Return of premium:** This rider enables the insured to receive the refund of premium paid (up to the percentages specified in the policy) if no or minimal claim was made. This is paid at a pre-determined time, as well as throughout the life of the policy.

11. **Lifetime benefit:** This enables the insured to be paid for as long they are totally disabled, if disability occurs before age 65

and they are totally disabled until age 65.

12. **Accidental death and dismemberment rider:** This rider provides a lump sum payment for accidental loss of life, foot or hand.

13. **Health care profession rider:** This rider provides monthly disability benefit payments to the insured health care professional who contracts HIV, Hepatitis B or Hepatitis C in the course of their day-to-day duties and regulations, or legislation prohibits them from carrying out their duties.

Disability Insurance for Self-Employed

The average self-employed person oftentimes has no group benefit. The financial responsibilities of self-

employed persons go beyond
themselves and their immediate
families. The suppliers, customers,
creditor's employees, and partners also
depend on their ability to work and to
generate income. Good financial
planning can save the self-employed
person's business. When they cannot
work, bills pile up regardless of a
disability. Bills can eat up RRSP,
business equity, investments and even
home equity if a self-employed person
were to become disabled without any
form of protection. Creditors can force
such self-employed person into
receivership. To prevent scenarios like
this, sound planning would see a self-
employed person have disability
insurance to cover the following:
   a. Income
   b. Business overhead
   c. Pay off deferred income taxes
   d. Pay off bank loan or at the
      minimum of the associated
      interest

Businesses in partnerships can buy disability insurance on each partner in the proportion of their participation in the business.

Businesses with a key person can also buy disability insurance on such a person. Corporations can also buy disability insurance on the directors who are heavily involved in the running of the business.

Group Insurance Plans

Group insurance plans provide about 4.6 million Canadians with short-term disability protection and about 10 million Canadians with long-term disability insurance.

A typical group plan provides three different levels of coverage:

1. **Sick leave:** This is usually at no cost to the employee. It is often provided by the employer. Sick leave enables an employee to receive full pay for a short period

of time (usually few days to a few weeks, depending on the employer's policy) if they are injured or ill.

2. **Short Term Disability (STD):** Most short-term disability provides a percentage of the employee's normal earnings, for example, 70% up to a certain length of time. Short-term disability can range in duration from 15 weeks, 26 weeks to 52 weeks. Short-term disability is paid after the Employment Insurance (EI) disability benefit runs out.

3. **Long-Term Disability (LTD):** This coverage starts when the short-term disability runs out (if available, depending on the duration). Long-term disability typically replaces 60-70% of the employee's normal income, often expressed in dollars (for example, $6,000 per

month). Long-term disability
benefits are usually reduced or
offset by disability payments
from Canada Pension Plan
(CPP), Quebec Pension Plan
(QPP), or worker compensation
board (WCB).

Special Purpose Plans

These are some special purpose plans
in some situations:

1. **Auto Insurance:** In the event of
   an auto accident that results in
   injury. In most provinces, the
   auto insurance provider is
   usually the first and second
   payer of disability benefits. This
   means the auto insurance
   provider would pay first
   disability benefit before any
   other plan kicks in, or they
   would pay net after another plan
   is paid.

2. **Creditor's Insurance:** Banks
   and loan companies provide this
   type of disability insurance on

mortgages, bank loans, car loans/financing, lines of credit, student credit, credit cards and similar loans. Creditor's insurance covers loan payments usually for a certain amount of time.

3. **Dismemberment Coverage:** Dismemberment coverage would pay a lump sum for full or partial loss or use of a limb, hearing or vision.

4. **Travel Insurance:** Travel insurance covers all types of risk, from trip cancellation to emergency hospital, medical costs, loss of baggage, companion travel insurance, or accidental death insurance.

5. **Life insurance:** One of the riders on a life insurance policy is the disability waiver of premium, this allows the insured to stop making premium payments while disabled for at

least six months, and thus keep the policy.

6. **Long-term care**: In the event that the insured cannot independently complete two of five activities of daily living, the insurer would pay the insured the pre-determined sum of insurance after the pre-determined waiting period (30 to 90 days).

CHAPTER FIVE
Long-Term Care Insurance
(If I Need Help for Myself Insurance)

Why Long-Term Care Insurance (LTCI)?

The chances of living to 100 years of age are better now than ever before. Due to long living, life comes with many more twists and turns that many clients are not financially prepared for. Fast forward the next 35 years. As baby boomers age, the cost of providing long-term insurance to the elderly in Canada will be $1.2 trillion, and only about half of that is covered by government programs. By 2036, it is expected that 25% of the population will be over 65 years old with almost 1 million Canadians afflicted with dementia.

As mentioned above, many Canadians are not financially prepared for their long-term care needs. Many think that full time care in a long-term care facility (commonly referred to as senior home or nursing home) will be fully paid by government health care programs. Unfortunately, long-term care is not covered by the public health care system. In reality, depending on a person's circumstance, the government health care programs may cover only a small part of the costs for a nursing home or other specialized residential care facility, or maybe none. This means that the person would pay a significant portion of the cost associated with long-term care out of pocket-savings, pensions, selling homes or taking out equity, selling investments, etc.

According to a Leger Marketing survey conducted on behalf of the CLHIA, almost three quarters of

Canadians (74%) admit they have no financial plan to pay for long term care if the need arises. More often, when long-term care is mentioned many people think of the aged and the need for a nursing home. It is difficult to imagine when we are young and healthy that at some point in the future, our health situation could change and we could require specialized ongoing care from another person. However, there are some situations that could make an otherwise healthy, independent, young person to require long-term care. A sudden debilitating illness or an accident could lead to a 24/7 care for all ages.

What is Long-Term Care Insurance?

Essentially, long-term care insurance provides financial protection in the event that the insured is unable to care for one-selves due to a chronic illness, disability, congestive impairment such as dementia, or other age-related conditions that prevent them from independently carrying out any two of the six activities of daily living. The payment can be used to cover the cost of nursing homes and similar facilities, to hire a caregiver, or to be spent as they deem fit.

Generally speaking, there are two types of long-term care insurance:

a. **Income style plan:** This plan provides a pre-determined income to the insured in the event they cannot independently complete any two of the six activities of daily living (ADLs).

b. **Expenses reimbursement style plan:** This plan reimburses the expenses that are outlined in the plan, like private nursing services or homemaking, up to a pre-determined maximum.

Waiting Period

LTCI usually has a waiting period of between 30 -180 days. The waiting period is the period between when an event that triggers a claim happens, to the time the claims can be made.

For long-term care insurance the waiting period is the period between the time the client cannot independently carry out two activities of day living and the time claim can be made, the shorter the waiting period, the higher the premium. For clients with tiny retirement funds and little to no pension, the shorter waiting period is more appropriate.

Benefit Period

Benefit period refers to the duration the insured wants to get the payment in the event of a claim. The shorter the benefit period, the lower the premium. The common benefit periods are 100 weeks, 150 weeks, 250 weeks and unlimited.

Riders of LTCI

The common riders on long term care insurance are as follows:

1. **Return of premium on death:** This rider ensures that all eligible premiums are returned to the named beneficiary of the insured upon death. Please see the illustration from the insurer to determine what is to be returned.

2. **Inflation Protection:** Due to the effect of inflation on the purchasing power of the dollar an insured person could choose to have inflation protection, so as to guarantee that they would be paid a higher dollar amount (to neutralize the effect of inflation) in the future. Inflation protection could be either of these two options:

a. 2% compounded annually increasing to 3% while on claim: This means that the insured amount would increase by 2% annually while not on claim and 3% if the client were to be on claim.

b. 3% compounded annually while on claim: With this option, the insured amount remains the same until the client goes on claim at which time the benefit would increase annually by 3%.

3. **Waiver of premium benefits:** No premium paid while on claim; this rider can also be built into the base plan depending on the insurer

4. **Shared benefit:** This rider enables the insured and spouse/common law partner to

share the benefit. It is also referred to as pool coverage.

Types and Cost of Long-Term Care

Long-term care could be provided at

- A facility: A specialized residential care facility.
- A home: Either by family members or professional service.

Long-term care insurance can be provided by:

1. Professionals: Trained health care workers.
2. Family: Children, parents, brothers, sisters or any other related family members.
3. Friends: neighbors, friends, co-workers, etc.

Long-term care facility
Accommodation in a typical long-term care facility ranges from $900-$5,000

per month, depending on the following:

1. Type of room/facility.
2. Level of government funding available.
3. Level of care needed.
4. Province and city.

Home care

Private home care service costs range from $12 to $90 per hour for home making, personal care or nursing care. The cost varies from one province to the other.

Typical Cost of Care

Cost of long-term care in Canada ranges from $35,000 to $65,000 a year, depending on the level of care required and province of residency.

Long-term care insurance

There are many life and health insurance companies in Canada that provide long-term care insurance. Please contact a qualified financial advisor, preferably a Certified Financial Planner (CFP) to help you choose the appropriate amount of long-term care insurance.

In reviewing your application for long-term care insurance, the insurance company takes into account the following:

1. **Age:** At the time of the application. The younger you are, the lower the premium.
2. **Health:** The state of health when the application was submitted. The healthier you are, the lower your premium.
3. **Waiting period:** The longer the waiting period, the lower the premium and vice versa.
4. **Type and amount applied for:** Typically, the income style option costs more. Also, the higher the benefit applied for, the higher the cost.

5. **Riders:** The more options you choose, the higher the premium.

When will benefits be paid?

Typical benefits are paid monthly when the insured can no longer perform two of the six ADLs without support. The reasons for not being able to perform the ADLS may be due to illness, injury or loss of mental capacity. The ADLs are:

1. *Dressing*
2. *Bathing*
3. *Toileting*
4. *Eating*
5. *Maintaining continence*
6. *Transferring (moving out of bed or to bed, moving from chair to chair, etc.)*

When an insured cannot perform any two of the six ADLs, a claim should be filed with the insurer. The insurer will assess such a claim to determine the credibility. Additional reports or information may be obtained from a doctor or other health care professional.

CHAPTER SIX
Personal Health Insurance
(Medical, dental and prescription drugs insurance)

Personal health insurance helps to lower the risk of being financially burdened by expenses of preventive care or medical bills, as a result of an accident or illness. The provincial health plans provide coverage for many health expenses, but there are some gaps that can have some significant financial impact.

Depending on the province or territory of residency, Canadians would have to pay for;

1. Emergency medical services provided in another country.
2. Services provided by practitioners like chiropractors, massage therapists, or physiotherapists to promote

wellness or help with injury
recovery.
3. Medical equipment to assist
with mobility or well-being.
4. Prescription drugs to treat a
chronic or serious health
conditions.
5. Preventive or elective dental
care.
6. Vision care.
7. Preferred hospital
accommodation, etc.

Who should buy Personal Health Insurance?

The public health care fund is
continuously being re-assessed.
Government reduces the coverage of
some health care services and ceases to
provide others; hence more
responsibility is placed on Canadians
to pay out of pocket for routine health
related services that the government
health insurance plans do not cover,
such as vision care, prescription drugs,

dental care, preferred hospital accommodation, registered specialists and therapists.

Personal health insurance should be considered by any of the following categories of people:

1. People losing their group coverage or in between jobs.
2. People who do not have any group benefit such as self-employed persons, contractors, seasonal workers, part time worker, etc.
3. People who want additional coverage.
4. People who do not have health benefits through the employer, like casual staff, on call staff or even fulltime staff.
5. Professionals not covered by employer's plan.
6. Students.

What is covered by Personal Health Insurance?

The following are typically provided in a personal health insurance:

1. **Prescription drugs:** Most personal health insurance covers the cost of prescription drugs up to a certain limit. (Please ask your broker) Some deductibles could also apply, depending on the policy.

2. **Dental services:** If selected, the cost of routine dental care and emergency dental care is usually covered. Depending on the plan, some other dental care may be covered. Deductibles may also be applied (check with your broker).

3. **Preferred Hospital Accommodation:** The cost of private or semi-private hospital

accommodation is usually covered in the personal plan, if selected.

4. **Vision Care:** Prescription lenses and frames, contact lenses and laser eye surgery, and optometrist visits are usually covered, if vision care is selected.

5. **Registered Specialists and Therapists:** The cost associated with services provided by registered specialists and therapists like chiropractors, podiatrists, massage therapists, naturopaths, chiropodists, psychologists, physiotherapists, speech therapist, acupuncturists, etc. depending on the plan.

6. **Extended Health Benefits:** The cost associated with services like air ambulance,

emergency ambulance, and medical appliances, foot care, occupational therapy, private duty nursing, orthopedic shoes, assisted care, blood pressure monitors, hearing aid, etc. are usually covered, depending on the plan.

7. **Accidental death and dismemberment:** Usually an elective feature of a plan.

8. **Home care and Nursing:** Covers the cost of medical care provided in the insured home by a registered nurse, registered practical nurse, occupational therapist, certified home support worker, registered dietician, registered nursing assistant or health care aid.

9. **Accidental dental:** Covers the cost of accidental dental.

10. **Travel:** Emergency travel is covered under most plans.

11. **Survivor Benefit:** coverage is provided for one year to the dependent following the death of an adult policy owner.

Tax advantages

Professionals, self-employed persons, small business owners and corporation owners may be able deduct the premiums paid for their personal health insurance coverage from their annual income. If deductible, the coverage of these categories of people virtually pays for itself, as it can be treated as a business expenses. There could be some other tax implications, like tax benefits.

Please consult, your broker and your accountant before making a decision.

I can help!

Options (Plan Design)

Personal health insurance has many options depending on the desired coverage.

Plan can include or exclude dental plans, prescription drugs, hospital accommodation, vision care, etc. Clients also have option to pick a deductible range if they want to accommodate their needs and budgets. An advisor is the best resource to guide and help clients to select the most suitable plan for their needs and budgets.

CHAPTER SEVEN
Group Insurance Plan
(*Attract the Best Insurance*)

Group insurance plans are a way for an employer to keep their employees happy. The following are some of the reasons why group insurance can help a company:

A. **Protect the Business:** Group disability, health and dental plans ensure the company is not liable in the event that an employee becomes injured or sick.

B. **Attract and Retain Key and Top Talent:** A well-designed group benefit package can help a business to be more competitive in recruiting and retaining top talents. It also helps to boost employee satisfaction and maintain productivity.

C. **Compensation:** Employee benefit plans can be designed to cover dental, prescription drugs and cost of day-to-day health care, using before tax income thus leaving more money in the employees' pockets.

D. **Maintain Productivity:** Employees with group insurance focus more on the job than those without. The Best Doctors or Employee Assistance Program can provide outside resources, support and tools that are needed to ensure that employees stay focused at work.

E. **Protect Your Employees:** Canada's public health care system does not cover everything. It does provide access to physicians, surgeons, diagnostic tests and emergency medical treatment, but does not cover prescription drugs, dental services, etc. The cost of some new drugs can be on the high side and may be more than the average employee's annual income.

A group benefits plan helps to ensure that employees and their dependents are adequately covered and protected. A group benefits plan can be tailored to meet the special needs of any company and the workforce. Every organization is unique by size, demographics, income and needs.

Type of Benefits

A. **Health Care and Dental Care benefits:** These benefits help employees to bridge the ever-increasing gap between provincial health insurance plans and the coverage the employee and their family needs. Plan members have access to dental care, prescription drugs and extended health coverage should the need arise.

B. Life, Accidental Death and Dismemberment benefits:

These benefits provide employees and their family members with the needed financial support, in the event of a death or a tragic accident. Life, accidental death and dismemberment benefits help employees to prepare for the unexpected. Many plans also allow dependents (spouse and children) to be covered. Life, accidental death and dismemberment benefits allow plan members to buy more optional coverage, with medical test required in most cases.

C. **Disability benefits:** Short-term and long-term disability insurance help employers to pay an employee for the time taken off work and also afford the employer to hire a replacement without any increased cost. Disability comes with a flexible elimination period (waiting period), benefit period, disability definition (occupation) benefit amounts and cost of living adjustments.

D. **Critical Illness benefits:** Employees are paid a pre-determined lump sum of money in the event that they suffer from any of the covered illnesses such as cancer, stroke, etc. depending on the plan design.

E. **Vision Care benefits:** Cost of prescribed lenses, frames and eye examinations are included in a vision care benefit. The flexibility of vision benefits allows a plan owner to select the coverage amount.

F. **Health Spending Account benefit:** A health spending account benefit provides reimbursement for a wide variety of health-related expenses over and above regular benefit plans. Health spending account allows plan sponsors or owners to allocate health spending account credits into each plan member's account every year.

Participation
- ✓ *Mandatory Plan:* All eligible employees must participate in the plan.
- ✓ *Non-Mandatory Plan:* Some eligible employees can elect not

to participate in the plan, but most plans would require 75% participation of the plan population.

✓ *Contributory Plan:* Employees have to pay certain portions of the benefit premium depending on the plan design. Pay stubs of the employees would show money taken out of their pay for their benefits.

✓ *Non-Contributory plan:* Employees are not paying any portion of the plan benefits premium, it is 100% covered by the employer.

Eligibility

Most plans stipulate a waiting period for a new employee before they can be eligible for benefits under the group plan. Once coverage is in effect, it continues for as long as the employee is working for the employer and as long as the required premium contribution is made. If employment is terminated the employee has 31 days to convert group plan coverage into an individual policy.

CHAPTER EIGHT

Is Real Estate or Participating Whole Life as an Alternative Investment?
(Put Your Money to Work)

The goal of every investor is to maximize the profitability of their portfolio. This chapter will compare the cost and benefits of real estate investment and the participating whole life policy. Real estate is a traditional investment that many investors see as a hedge against inflation. It is believed that the value of a piece of real estate appreciates over time.

Costs of owning real estate

For the purpose of this illustration, the value of the real estate and participating policy to be used would be $500,000 each. The following are the estimated costs of owning a $500,000 rental property.

1. **Down payment:** At 20% down payment for rental property, the down payment for a $500,000 property would be $100,000.

2. **Closing cost:** At estimated 1.5%, the cost for a $500,000 property would be $7500. The actual closing cost may exceed the estimated 1.5% used by most financial institutions.

3. **Cost of advertisement and showing:** The cost of advertising the house for rent and showing the house to potential rentals is estimated at $500.

4. **Cost of maintenance and repairs:** At an estimated annual cost of 1.5% (not adjusted to inflation), the cost of

maintenance and repairs to the property over 20 years is $150,000 ($7,500 X 20) or $7500 annually.

5. **Cost of collecting rents:** The direct cost of collecting rents (property management fees), including the cost estimate of collecting overdue rent and the attendant cost of appearance on the rental board. At 10% of the estimated $2,200 per month rent or $26,400 estimated cost of collecting rent over a 20-year window, $2,640 x 20 = $52,800.

6. **Cost of Sales:** At 7% costs of sales, the estimated cost of sales, assuming the property value has doubled over a 20-year window (to $1 million) is $70,000.

7. **Cost of Property Insurance:** The cost of insuring the property, assuming a straight cost of $100 per month for 20 years is $24,000.

8. **Property tax:** Assuming no increase in property tax, and assuming an annual tax bill of $5000 the estimated property tax bill is $100,000.

9. **Sundry cost:** This would include things like unpaid rent, property tax increases, and increase in the cost of maintenance and repairs, cost of utility when the house is vacant, etc. estimated at $20,000 over the 20 years period or $1,000 per annum.

10. **Mortgage payment:** With an estimated mortgage of $400,000, the monthly

mortgage payment, assuming an interest rate of 2.59% over a 20-year window is $2,134.34 per month or $512,241.60 for 20 years. The total cost estimated ($100,000 + $7500 + $500 + $150,000 + $52,800 + $70,000 + $24,000 + $100,000 + $20000 + $512,241.60) is $1,037,041.60.

Benefits of Real Estate

A real estate is a physical asset and the owner derives pride of ownership from a real estate, as well as rent from tenants. The real estate is also expected to increase in value over time.

The benefits of a real estate include:

1. *Rents:* Estimated at $2,200 over a 20-year window, and year - round occupancy (no vacancy), the estimated benefit to the owner is $528,000.

2. *Increase in value:* With an estimated 3.5% increase in values year after year, a piece of real estate is expected to double in value over a 20-year period. Using our example of a $500,000 property, the property is expected to be worth $1 million in 20 years' time.

Cost Associated with a Participating Life Insurance

The cost of owning a participating life insurance assuming a 40-year-old male is as follows:

1. **Cost of underwriting:** The total cost of underwriting is borne by the insurance company. There is no cost implication to the insured. However, the investor is expected to be in a reasonable state of health.

2. **Premium:** For a $500,000 20-year payment period participating life insurance, using Equitable Life estate max. 20, the annual payment is $13,210. The cost of insurance over a 20-year period for a standard life (no increase applicable) is $13,210 x 20 = $264,200.

Benefit to the investor

The investor is expected to be in a reasonable state of health, and qualify for the insurance upon application. Once the insurance is issued, the investor has immediately put in place a $500,000 value into their estate as long as the premium is paid until the date. The $500,000 is fully paid for any time a death happens, or in 20 years' time.

The benefit to the investor includes:

1. **Life insurance:** The investor has $500,000 life insurance from the day the insurance is approved.

2. **The cash surrender values:** At a 2016 dividend scale with equitable life insurance Company of Canada, the estimated cash surrender values of a $500,000 par policy after 20 years is $437,378 with a death benefit of $900,186.

Tax Implications

Real Estate

The various costs incurred in the real estate investment, like the down payment, mortgage payments, property tax payments, maintenances and repairs are after tax dollars. Capital gain tax (presently at 50%) is also due when the property that is not designated as a principal residency is sold. From the example above, the adjusted cost base (ACB) of the property is cost price ($500,000) plus cost of sales ($70,000), plus the estimated cost of repair only ($50,000), not the cost of upgrades or the cost of $620,000 while the fair market price (FMP) is expected to be $1,000,000. The profit is $1,000,000 - $620,000 = $380,000.

Depending on the tax bracket of the investor, the investor may incur a tax

bill of ($380,000/ 50% x .40) $76,000.
The cash flow from rent is also taxable
in the hand of the investor. The
allowable deductions include the
insurance premium, repairs, mortgage
interest and cost of utilities.

Participating life insurance

The only cost of a participating life
insurance is the monthly premium. The
premium is paid from after-tax income
or from a corporate account. The
investor can also assign the cash
surrender value to a bank as collateral,
in order to minimize their tax liability
if they need to take out the money. The
death benefit is also not taxable, since
the premiums paid are from after-tax
money.

CONCLUSION

Investment in real estate is commonly referred to as passive investment by many. However, it may be time consuming depending on the types of tenants, the state of the economy, the building types, the size of the real estate portfolio, location etc.

While, investments in participating life insurance can be described in entity as passive investment, no further activity is required apart from paying the premiums as of, when due.

Investments in real estate may also include some risk retention even when the property is insured, for example, if the property were to be vacant there would be no cash flow and yet expenses may continue on the property sudden damages or repair needs are also some of the uncertainties surrounding investments in real estate.

With participating life insurance, there are no repairs, no damages and no vacancy. The life insurance risk is totally borne by the insurer. I find investment in participating life insurance less risky, less time consuming and more rewarding.

If you need assistance, you can book a non - obligatory consultation service at www.valuesfinacial.ca. Remember it is prudent to act swiftly in this regard. You buy insurance with your health and pay for it with your money. Drastic or further changes in your health may sometimes mean ineligibility to have insurance. *A stitch in time saves nine.* **I can help!**

I AM A Life Insurance Policy

The importance of life insurance (Health insurance inclusive) was fittingly described by an unknown author as follows.

- o I am a piece of paper, a drop of ink and a few cents of premium.
- o I am a promise to pay.
- o I help people see visions, dream dreams and achieve economic immortality.
- o I am education to the children.
- o I am savings.
- o I am a property that increases in values from year to year.
- o I lend money when you need it most, with no questions asked or credit check.
- o I pay off mortgages, so that the family can remain together in their own homes.

- I assure people the daring to live and moral right to die.
- I create money where none existed before.
- I am the great emancipator from want.
- I guarantee the continuity of business.
- I conserve the employer's investment.
- I am tangible evidence that a man is a good husband and father, and a woman a good wife and mother.
- I am a declaration of financial independence and economic freedom.
- I am the difference between an old man or woman and an elderly gentleman or lady.
- I provide cash if illness, injury, old age or death cuts off the breadwinner's income.
- I am the only thing that you can buy on the installment plan that

your family doesn't have to finish paying for.

- o I am protected by laws that prevent creditors from assessing the money I give to the loved ones.
- o I bring dignity, peace of mind and security to your family.
- o I supply investment capital that makes the wheels turn and the motors hum.
- o I guarantee the financial ability to have happy holidays and the laughter of children even though father or mother is not there.
- o I am the guardian angel of the home.
- o I am life {and health} insurance.